Steck-Vaughn/Berrent

ESPA *Success*

Level C

in Language Arts Literacy

Estelle Kleinman

Acknowledgments

Editorial Manager: Karen Bischoff

Senior Editor: Amy Losi

Editors: Caren Churchbuilder
Debra Tursi

Design Director: Steven Coleman

Design and Layout: Jan Jarvis/Willow Graphics

Design Associate: Jean-Paul Vest

Illustrations: Claudette St. Pierre

Grateful acknowledgment is made to the following for permission to use copyrighted material:

"This Is Just to Say" by William Carlos Williams, from *Collected Poems: 1909-1939, Volume I.* Copyright © 1938 by New Directions Publishing Corp. Reprinted by permission of New Directions Publishing Corp.

"The Thought That Counted" by Peggy Noll, *Highlights for Children*, February 2000. Copyright © 2000 by Highlights for Children, Inc., Columbus, Ohio. Reprinted by permission.

"Kite" from *More Beginning Crafts for Beginning Readers* by Alice Gilbreath. Copyright © 1976 by Alice Gilbreath. Published by Modern Curriculum Press, an imprint of Pearson Learning. Used by permission.

"A Gift for Tía Rosa" by Karen T. Taha. Copyright © 1986 by Karen T. Taha. Reprinted by permission of the author.

"Hide and Seek: Disappearing Coin Trick" from *Magic Fun*, by the editors of *Owl* magazine. Copyright © 1991 by Greey de Pencier Books. Reprinted by permission of Little, Brown and Company.

"The Pasture" from *The Poetry of Robert Frost* edited by Edward Connery Lathem. Copyright © 1939, 1967, 1969 by Henry Holt and Company, LLC. Reprinted by permission of Henry Holt and Company, LLC.

The ESPA is published by the New Jersey Department of Education. Such organization has neither endorsed nor authorized this test-preparation book.

STECK-VAUGHN
BERRENT

A Harcourt Company

www.steck-vaughn.com

ISBN 0-7398-2343-4

1 2 3 4 5 6 7 8 9   B   05 04 03 02 01 00

Table of Contents

Preface

Tests are a necessary way to measure your success as a learner. The materials in this book have been carefully prepared to help you learn the skills you will need to succeed on the ESPA in Language Arts Literacy.

The first two units give you the tools for reading, writing, and answering questions. These units present instruction and practice, as well as steps for you to follow when answering test questions. The last unit is a practice test that uses all the skills taught in this book.

This book will give you the help you need to do well on the ESPA in language arts literacy.

Writing might seem scary to you. After all, it is not easy to put your ideas down on paper. You will feel less afraid if you think of writing as a process. This means that there is a special set of steps to follow. Good writers move back and forth among these steps. Here are the steps of the writing process:

The Writing Process

Prewriting

Choose your topic, audience, and purpose; plan your writing.

Drafting

Start writing; don't worry about making mistakes. Get a beginning, middle, and ending down on paper.

Revising/Editing

Read your writing. Does it meet your purpose? Are your ideas clear? Check for mistakes in spelling, grammar, and punctuation.

Presenting

Share your writing.

CHAPTER One
Prewriting Strategies

Getting Started

Before you begin writing, ask yourself these questions:

◆ What should I write about?

◆ Why am I writing?

◆ Who will read my writing?

What Should I Write About?

Sometimes your teacher will tell you what to write about. Other times, you will have to think of a topic on your own. Ideas for writing topics can come from many places. Where can you find these ideas? They are right inside your head! To find them, you might want to use one of these ways:

◆ **Freewriting** *Freewriting* means that you write for several minutes without stopping. Just jot down anything and everything that comes into your mind.

◆ **Brainstorming** When you freewrite, you are on your own. But you *brainstorm* in a group. Get together with some classmates and share ideas. You'll be surprised how quickly one idea leads to another.

◆ **Making an idea web** Start by circling a word or phrase in the center of a blank paper. Then add other ideas around it. Surround each of those with other ideas. In this way, you'll create groups of ideas. Look at the following idea web on the circus.

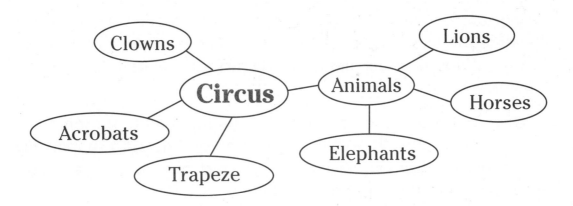

From this web, you can choose a topic. For example, you might decide to write about the animals at the circus. Circus animals are elephants, horses, and lions.

Follow THROUGH...

1. Imagine that you have a pen pal. Your pen pal lives in another country. You want to think of interesting things to write in your letters to him or her. Your pen pal might like to hear about your life, what your school is like, and what it is like to live in the United States. Using freewriting, brainstorming, or an idea web, come up with the five topics for letters to your pen pal.

Making a Plan

When you put a model airplane together, you follow a plan. The same is true of writing. You have to plan before you write. You need to order your ideas about your topic.

The first step is to decide on a main idea. The main idea is the all-important key point that you want to get across to your readers. Try to state this main idea in one sentence. For example, a main idea for a report about hamsters might be "Hamsters make good pets because they are fun and easy to care for."

Once you have your main idea, you might need to do some fact finding. Ask yourself, "What information do I need to support my main idea?" After you have done your fact finding, you can decide how to order your supporting details.

One way to put your ideas in order is to make a time line. You write down events in the same way in which they happened.

Another way to plan your story is to use a Venn diagram. A Venn diagram compares two things. When you compare things, you show how they are alike and how they are different. In a Venn diagram you can do both. It is made from two circles. Each circle represents one of the things you want to compare. List what is different about each thing in the outer parts of the circles. List what is alike about the things inside, where the circles come together.

◆ **Making a time line** A time line is used in many ways. It can help you write down events in the order in which they happened. For example, you can write down what happened first, next, and last. You can use a time line to help you plan a story. You can write down what happens in the beginning, middle, and ending of the story. Look at this time line for planning a birthday party.

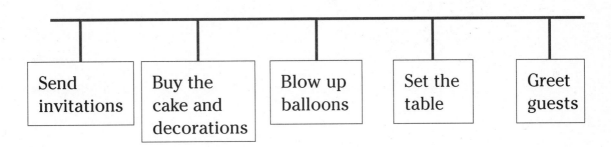

| Send invitations | Buy the cake and decorations | Blow up balloons | Set the table | Greet guests |

Follow THROUGH

2. **Think about what you do from the time you wake up until the time you enter your classroom. Write a time line showing the things you do each morning in the order in which you do them.**

◆ **Making a Venn diagram** A Venn diagram is used to compare two things. The following Venn diagram compares lions and tigers.

LION
- Lives in Africa
- Has yellowish-brown stripes
- Lives in groups or alone

BOTH
- Are about 10 feet long
- Live 20-25 years

TIGER
- Lives in Asia
- Has tannish-yellow with black stripes
- Lives alone

Follow THROUGH

3. Use a Venn diagram to compare any two things you choose. Here are some possibilities: characters in a story, types of toys, sports, places, or movies.

CHAPTER TWO
Drafting

Caught in the Draft

Drafting means writing your ideas in sentences and paragraphs. Getting started can be the hardest part of writing. Imagine that you are writing to a friend. Remember, you already have a plan. That is what the prewriting stage was all about. And you can always make changes later on.

Building a Good Paragraph

A paragraph is more than just a list of sentences with the first line indented. The sentences in a paragraph support a single main idea. The paragraph may even have a topic sentence. A topic sentence states the main idea. Each detail supports the main idea like building blocks.

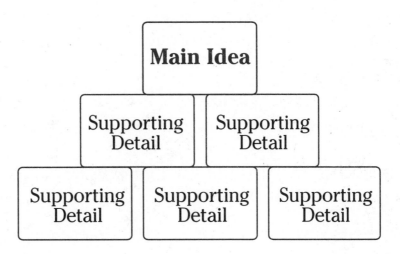

Sticking Together

Take another look at the building blocks. What do you think will happen if we don't add cement to make the building blocks stick together? It won't be long before everything comes tumbling down.

In a similar way, the sentences in a paragraph must stick together. Supporting the main idea is not enough. The sentences must also be clearly connected.

How do you make the supporting details "stick together"?

◆ Repeat a key word.

◆ Use synonyms.

◆ Use pronouns.

◆ Use words that tie ideas together.

Repeat a key word   Repeating a key word is a good way to link sentences in a paragraph. Here is an example:

My sister and I walked up to the beautiful gold **car** and peeked in. It was like no **car** we had ever owned.

Use synonyms   A *synonym* is a word that means about the same thing as another word. Using the same word too often can get boring. Try using a synonym instead. Notice how the synonyms below link the two sentences:

I thought that the gold car looked like a car for **rich** people. Only **wealthy** people could ride in such a grand car.

Use pronouns   You can also link sentences by using a pronoun for a key word, as in this example:

My **mother** didn't like the car. **She** wanted my father to take it back.

Use words that tie ideas together There are words and phrases that make links between sentences in a paragraph. Here are some common ones: *first, in addition, for example, because, but, however, in the same way, on the other hand.* Notice how one of these helps link these sentences:

My mother wouldn't ride in the car. **However,** she let me and my sister go for rides with my father.

Putting It All Together

Your paragraphs should work together to support your main idea. And each paragraph should flow smoothly into the next.

Here are some tips to help you while you are writing your draft:

◆ Relax! Nobody will see your first draft but you. Don't be afraid to make mistakes.

◆ Reread your prewriting notes and look at your plan. Use it as a guide for your writing.

◆ Keep these things in mind: your main idea, your audience, and your purpose.

Follow THROUGH

1. **Write one paragraph on any topic you choose. Make sure that it is a topic you know something about so you can add enough supporting details.**

CHAPTER Three
Revising and Editing

Revising Text

It is now time to polish your writing. You do this by *revising* your draft. When you revise, you check the content, organization, and wording. Reread your draft to see how you can make it better. Ask yourself these questions:

- ◆ Is the main idea clear?

- ◆ Are the ideas well organized?

- ◆ Do the sentences flow smoothly?

- ◆ Have I chosen words that clearly state my meaning?

To revise your draft, think about making these changes:

- ◆ Add information.

- ◆ Cut information.

- ◆ Move information.

- ◆ Combine sentences.

Add information Should you add something? Do your readers need more information? When you reread your first draft, you may decide that you left out something important. This is the time to add it.

Cut information Should you take something out? Have you included any facts or ideas that don't have anything to do with your main idea? Is something repeated? If so, get rid of it now.

ESPA Success in Language Arts Literacy ◆ LEVEL C

Move information   Should you move something? Is a word, sentence, or paragraph in the wrong place? Perhaps the paragraphs aren't in the best order. Or maybe the sentences in the paragraph are out of order, and your meaning is not clear. Now is the time to make these changes.

Combine sentences   Do you have too many short, choppy sentences? If so, you might want to combine some sentences.

Look at this paragraph. Notice how it has been revised to improve the content.

When you talk, you may make many sounds. The way you pass air from your lungs over your vocal cords plays an important part in the way you make sound. To make most of these sounds, you must let air out of the parts of your body called the lungs. As the air leaves your lungs, it must pass over parts of your body called vocal cords. The air makes your vocal cords move back and forth. This makes sounds. You can make loud sounds ~~You make loud sounds~~ by forcing a lot of air to pass over your vocal cords. You can change to a softer sound by passing less air over them. ~~Sometimes your vocal cords get strained from too much talking.~~

Your lungs, found in your chest, are used for breathing air.

Follow THROUGH...

1. **Revise these paragraphs. Use the suggestions you have just read about.**

Even though Dolphins live in the water, they are not fish. They are warm-blooded animals. They take in and let out air through a blowhole on top of their heads. Unlike fish, dolphins must come to the surface of the water to get air.

Dolphins live together in groups called schools. They are loving mates. They make good parents. The female dolphin has only one baby at a time. Like babies of other warm-blooded animals, a baby dolphin is born live. The mother dolphin feeds her baby milk and watches over it with the father's help. Dolphins have about 200 teeth in all.

Follow These Steps

As you think about how to revise the draft, keep these questions in mind:

- ◆ Do I need to add any information?
- ◆ Do I need to cut any information?
- ◆ Would the text read better if I move some information?
- ◆ Should I combine any sentences?

ESPA Success in Language Arts Literacy ◆ LEVEL C

Editing Text

When you revise, you look for the big things. After you've done this, you check the details by *editing* your work. Before you share your writing with readers, check it for mistakes in grammar, spelling, and punctuation.

When editing your writing, keep the rules of grammar in mind. Here are a few things to look for when checking your work:

1. Make sure that each verb agrees with, or matches, its subject in number.

   Wrong: The dog and cat **is** hungry.

   Right: The dog and cat **are** hungry.

2. Make sure the correct pronouns are used.

   Wrong: Juan and **me** played ball.

   Right: Juan and I played ball.

3. Avoid double negatives. These are sentences with two negative words.

   Wrong: He **didn't** say **nothing**.

   Right: He **didn't** say **anything**.

You should also ask yourself these questions:

◆ Did I spell all the words correctly?

◆ Did I capitalize the correct words?

◆ Is the punctuation correct: end punctuation, commas, apostrophes, and quotation marks?

Spelling

Your goal as a writer is to present your ideas to your readers. But if you misspell many words, your ideas may be lost. That is why it is important to keep a dictionary handy to check your spelling. It is also a good idea to have someone you trust look at your work for spelling mistakes.

Many English textbooks contain a list of words that are easy to misspell. You might want to study them. These textbooks might also provide spelling rules for you to review.

There are many ways that you can improve your spelling. As you write, pay attention to any words you have trouble spelling. Write these words down in a notebook. Then, try these simple steps to learn to spell each word.

Say it Look at the word, and say it out loud. Then, say it again. Be sure to pronounce each syllable.

Imagine it Without looking at the word, imagine seeing it in your mind. Try to picture the word spelled correctly.

Write it Look at the word and write it. Then, write it again without looking at the printed word.

Check it Check what you have written against the printed word. Did you spell the word correctly? If not, go back to step 1.

Follow THROUGH

2. Correct all of the spelling mistakes you find in this paragraph.

Seed plants are importent to people in many ways. One of these ways is that seed plants are ofen used for food. People eet parts of many seed plants. Aples and corn are parts of seed plants. People also use parts of seed plantz to make food. Bread is one sutch food. Bred is made from parts of wheat plants.

Capitalization

When you edit, you should also look for mistakes in capitalization. You should check for capitalization of sentences, proper nouns, and proper adjectives.

Capitalization of Sentences

1. Capitalize the first word in a sentence.

Half of the moon is always in sunlight.

2. Capitalize the first word in a direct quotation—a person's exact words.

Toby asked, "**W**ho was the first person to walk on the moon?"

Capitalization of Proper Nouns

A proper noun is a particular person, place, or thing. Capitalize all proper nouns, such as these:

1. Names and words used as names

George **W**ashington   **M**other **T**eresa   **M**om

2. Titles that come before names

Dr. Mott   **C**hief Sitting Bull   **S**enator Jackson

Capitalize the title only if the person's name follows (**M**ayor Ramos). If the name is not used, do not capitalize the title (we talked to the **m**ayor).

3. Names of particular groups of people

Canadians   **A**frican-**A**mericans   **B**lackfeet

4. Names of places, stars, and planets

   Pacific **O**cean   **M**exico   **N**orth **S**tar   **M**ars

5. Days of the week, months, and holidays

   Thursday   **J**une   **V**alentine's **D**ay

6. Names of businesses and particular products

   General **M**ills   **K**leenex   **J**ello

7. Organizations, colleges, and political parties

   Boy **S**couts of **A**merica   **R**utgers **U**niversity   **R**epublican

8. Events from history

   World **W**ar II   **B**oston **T**ea **P**arty   **U**nited **S**tates **C**ivil **W**ar

9. Religions and religious terms

   Christianity   **A**llah   **K**oran   **T**orah

10. Sections of a country or the world

    East **C**oast   **M**idwest   **S**outh **P**acific

11. First, last, and all the important words in a title

    Charlotte's Web (book)

    "**T**omorrow" (song)

    the *Jersey Journal* (newspaper)

Capitalization of Proper Adjectives

Capitalize adjectives formed from proper nouns. These are called proper adjectives.

African studies   **C**anadian border   **J**ewish holidays

Follow THROUGH...

3. **Correct any mistakes in capitalization in this paragraph.**

Denzel was happy that it was friday. This weekend uncle Roy would be coming to visit. He was going to spend the labor day weekend with Denzel's family. Denzel's uncle always brings gifts. Last year, he gave Denzel a book called *The Most beautiful Place in the World*. It was about a poor boy named juan, who lived with his grandmother in guatemala. Denzel loved the book. He likes reading about american families, but he also likes reading about children from other countries.

Punctuation

End Punctuation

All sentences end with one of these:

◆ a period   ◆ a question mark   ◆ an exclamation point

Period   Use a period at the end of a statement, most commands, and requests.

Statement: The children played in the park.

Command: Clean your room.

Request: Please shut the door.

Question mark   Use a question mark at the end of a sentence that asks a question.

What time is it**?**

Exclamation point   Use an exclamation point at the end of a sentence that states a strong feeling.

What a good swimmer Alex is!

Comma

The comma helps the reader know when to rest. It can also be used to separate certain parts of the sentence. Here are ways to use a comma.

◆ Use a comma before *and*, *but*, or *or* when the word joins two complete thoughts.

The class read the story, and everyone liked it.

◆ Use a comma to separate three or more items in a series.

My aunt has cats, dogs, and birds.

◆ Use a comma after a word or word group that comes before the subject and verb at the beginning of a sentence.

Yes, you can go.

After all, it's still early.

When you get there, call me.

◆ Use commas to separate the parts of an address or a date.

Her address is 7 Hayes Avenue, East Brunswick, New Jersey 08816.

My brother was born on Monday, December 27, 1999.

◆ Use a comma to separate the speaker from his or her exact words in a direct quotation.

Lin said, "My dog can do many tricks."

◆ Use a comma to set off the name of a person spoken to in a sentence.

Alicia, how old are you?

Let me help you, Mr. Ames.

Apostrophe

Use an apostrophe to show possession (*John's bike*) and to form a contraction (*don't*). Here are some rules for using an apostrophe:

◆ Use an apostrophe and *–s* to form the possessive of a singular noun.

the girl's team, the bus's seats

◆ Use an apostrophe alone to form the possessive of a plural noun that ends in *–s*.

the boys' books, dogs' collars

◆ Use an apostrophe and *–s* to form the possessive of a plural noun that does not end in *–s*.

children's shows, men's shirts

◆ Use an apostrophe in place of letters left out of contractions. A contraction is a word made by joining two words and leaving out one or more letters.

can't (can not)   you're (you are)   it's (it is)

Keep in mind that the possessive for *it* is *its* (no apostrophe). The contraction *it's* (with an apostrophe) means *it is*.

Quotation Marks

Here are some things to keep in mind when you use quotation marks (" "):

◆ Use quotation marks before and after a direct quotation. Do not use quotation marks for an indirect quotation.

"I have two sisters," Carl said.
[These are Carl's exact words.]

Carl said that he has two sisters.
[These are not Carl's exact words.]

◆ Use quotation marks around titles of short works.

"The Lost Lake" (short story)

"The Pasture" (poem)

"Swimming with the Dolphins" (article)

◆ Always place a comma or period inside closing quotation marks.

"Let's go home," she said. He answered, "I have to stop at the store first."

Follow THROUGH...

4. **Some end punctuation and commas are missing from this paragraph. Write in the missing punctuation.**

Who was the greatest woman runner of all time Many people think it was Wilma Rudolph. Wilma was born in 1940 in Bethlehem Tennessee. She had a disease called polio. The doctor said that she would never walk but Wilma's family would not give up. They did exercises with her every day. By the age of twelve, she could walk without crutches braces, or special shoes. She started running and winning races at school track meets. In 1960, she ran in the Olympics Wilma set world records while winning three gold medals

Follow THROUGH

5. **Some apostrophes and quotation marks are missing from this passage. Write in the missing punctuation.**

There once was a great oak. The oaks strength was known far and wide. Smaller trees were bowed by the wind, but the oak didnt bend. This was not true of the reed. It bowed this way and that, whichever way the wind blew.

Why dont you stay still like I do?" said the oak to the reed.

"Im not as strong as you, said the reed.

One day a gale blew through the forest. The great oak refused to give way to the gales fierce winds. Soon the oak was blown to the ground.

The reeds fate was much better. It bent with the wind. Then it rose again fresh as ever.

The reed looked sadly at the oak. Then it said, "Poor oak, all your strength did you no good. You couldnt bend even if you wanted to.

CHAPTER Four
Writing to Speculate

Speculating About a Picture

On the ESPA you will be asked to speculate about a picture. The word *speculate* means "to guess." When you speculate, you use your imagination and what you know to decide what is going on in the picture. Your story must be based on the information you get from looking at the picture. Follow these steps:

Look at the picture Before you write anything, look at the picture. Think about these questions.

◆ What characters (people or animals) do you see in the picture?

◆ Where and when do you think the events in the picture are taking place?

◆ What do you see happening in the picture? What events do you think led up to this? What do you think will happen next?

Plan your thoughts You will be asked to write a story about what might be happening in the picture. In a story, a writer tells about one main idea. A story has characters, a plot (a series of events), and a setting (place and time). The plot has a problem and a solution. Before you write the story, you should plan your thoughts. You might want to take notes, create an idea web, or do other prewriting work. A good way to plan your ideas about a story is to use a story map, like the one below.

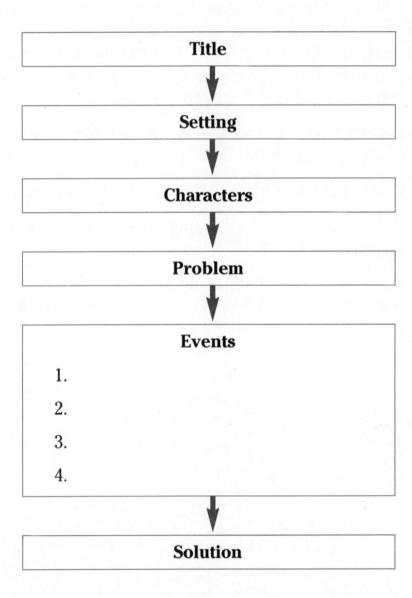

Write the story Use your prewriting work to write a story about what might be happening in the picture.

ESPA Success in Language Arts Literacy ◆ LEVEL C

Writing Task A

Use the picture on page 32 to write a story about what might be happening.

You may take notes, create an idea web, make a story map, or do other prewriting work on page 33. Then, write your story on page 34.

Here is a writing checklist to help you do your best writing. Before you begin writing, read the checklist.

Writer's Checklist

❑ Know your audience.

❑ Think about your topic and reason for writing.

❑ Show your audience that your point of view is correct.

❑ Support your point of view with details and other information.

❑ Organize your ideas so that they make sense.

❑ State your ideas clearly.

❑ Use different vocabulary words.

❑ Write neatly.

After you write your story, read it to yourself. Go over the checklist to make sure that your writing is the best it can be.

Follow These Steps   First, look at the picture. What is happening in the picture? When and where do you think it takes place? What are the people doing? What events do you think led up to this? What do you think will happen next? Jot down some notes or make a story map. Use your prewriting work to write a story about what you think is going on in the picture.

Writing Task A — Prewriting Space

Use this space to plan your writing.

Writing Task A

ESPA Success in Language Arts Literacy ◆ LEVEL C

CHAPTER Five
Writing to Explain

Writing an Explanation

When you explain something, you make it plain or clear. One activity on the test will ask you to write a composition. Your writing will be based on reading a poem.

Poetry is a special kind of writing. Poetry squeezes meaning into a small number of words and lines. Poetry invites the reader to look at the world in unusual ways. It uses language to suggest and compare things.

These steps will help you discover a poem's meaning:

Question   The words in poetry are often easy to read, but knowing what they mean can be difficult. As you read the poem, ask questions about the meaning. Sometimes you must use your imagination to figure it out.

Listen   Hear the musical nature of the words. The poet often chooses words that appeal to the senses. What pictures do these words create in your mind?

Make a list of events   Stop from time to time to list the events that have taken place so far. This is especially helpful for longer poems.

Reword   Put the poem into your own words. This will help you understand the meaning.

Think about the whole poem   After you have read the poem, think about all of the events. What did the poem say to you?

Directions: Read the poem, "This Is Just to Say," to yourself while it is read to you. Then, you will complete a writing task. Ideas from the poem may help you with your writing.

This Is Just to Say
by William Carlos Williams

I have eaten
the plums
that were in
the icebox

and which
you were probably
saving
for breakfast

Forgive me
they were delicious
so sweet
and so cold

Writing Task B

Has there ever been a time when you said you were sorry to someone for something you did? Maybe you said the wrong thing or you fought with a friend. Write a composition about it. Be sure to explain what you did or said, how you felt at the time, and what you learned from it.

You may take notes, create an idea web, or do other prewriting work in the space on page 39. Then, write your composition on the lines on page 40.

Use this checklist to help you do your best writing. Before you begin writing, read the checklist.

Writer's Checklist

❑ Know your audience.

❑ Think about your topic and reason for writing.

❑ Show your audience that your point of view is correct.

❑ Support your point of view with details and other information.

❑ Organize your ideas so that they make sense.

❑ State your ideas clearly.

❑ Use different vocabulary words.

❑ Write neatly.

After you write your composition, read it to yourself. Go over the checklist to make sure that your writing is the best it can be.

Follow These Steps   These steps will help you write your composition:

- Read the poem carefully. Use the steps you have learned in this chapter to help you understand its meaning.

- Look over the things you should include in your composition. Jot down some notes or use another prewriting steps to plan your thoughts.

- Think about how the poem might give you ideas for your writing.

- Decide on your main idea. State this main idea in one sentence and use this as your topic sentence.

- Think about how you want to plan your writing. Remember to include a beginning, middle, and ending.

- Write your composition, using your prewriting plan.

- Revise your work. Make sure that you have answered the questions completely. Then, edit for mistakes in grammar, spelling, and punctuation.

Writing Task B — Prewriting Space

Use this space to plan your writing.

Writing Task B

ESPA Success in Language Arts Literacy ◆ LEVEL C

Imagine taking a very strange airplane ride. The pilot has no idea where he is going or how he will get there. He pays no attention to the weather or air traffic. Instead, he puts the plane on automatic pilot and says, "I'm just going to sit back and enjoy the ride." What kind of a flight do you think you would have?

Just as a pilot needs a plan for flying, you need a plan for reading. You can be a better reader if you follow a few simple steps:

Set a purpose for reading   Be aware of why you are reading. This will help you decide how quickly to read and what to think about.

Make guesses   Before you read, look at the story: Read the title, flip through the pages, look at the pictures and headings (if any), and read a paragraph here and there. Then, make a guess as to what you will find in the story. Continue to make guesses as you read.

Ask questions   As you read, ask yourself questions about things you might not understand. Take time to think about answers to your questions. Then, reread parts of the story to try to figure out if your answers are correct.

Check your guesses   Keep your guesses in mind as you read. Are events turning out the way you expected? Make new guesses as you read more of the story. Continue until you have finished reading.

Narrative Text

What Is Narrative Text?

A *narrative* is text that tells a story. The story can be real or made up. Most narratives have certain parts in common:

◆ character   ◆ plot   ◆ setting   ◆ theme

Character   A character is a person or animal in a story. The reader learns about characters by what they say, do, and think. The reader can also learn about characters by what other characters say about them.

Plot   Plot is the series of events that make up a story. Usually, one of the characters in a plot has a problem. As the story develops, the problem grows. As you read, you see what is happening. The final part of the story tells how the problem is solved.

Setting   The setting is the time and place in which a story takes place. The time could be the past, present, or future. But the story might also tell you the year, the season, and even the time of day. The place may be a certain country, state, or neighborhood. The setting often helps set a mood. It may also play an important part in the plot.

Theme   The theme is the main idea of a narrative. It is an idea or message that the author wants to give to the reader.

Writing Tools

Narrative writers use certain tools in their writing. These include the following:

◆ comparisons

◆ imagery

◆ clues and hints

◆ symbols

◆ flashbacks

Comparisons   Writers use comparisons to make their writing come alive. Similes and metaphors are two kinds of comparisons. A writer may compare two unlike things, using the words *like* or *as* (The sun was like a big orange ball). This is called a *simile*. Or, a writer may describe something as though it were something else (The marshmallow cloud floated in the sky). This is called a *metaphor*.

Imagery   Writers may use words that suggest how someone or something looks, sounds, feels, smells or tastes. This is called *imagery*, because it puts an image, or picture, in the reader's mind.

Clues and hints   Writers may use clues or hints to suggest events that will take place later in the story. Clues and hints are used to build suspense. Another word for this is *foreshadowing*.

Symbols   A writer may use a person, place, thing, or event that stands for something else. A flag, for example, is a *symbol* for a country.

Flashback   A writer may stop the action of a story to tell about events that happened at an earlier time. This is called a *flashback* because the writer jumps back in time.

Directions: Read the story. Then, answer the questions that follow.

The Thought That Counted

by Peggy Noll

When my grandma lived with us, everything was not as nice as it seems on TV shows and in books. My grandma didn't smile much or bake gingersnap cookies. No. My grandma sat in her wheelchair all day long. When my kitten meowed, she yelled at him, "Scat!"

But I didn't start out to complain about Grandma. I

started out to tell the story of the amazing thing that happened at her last birthday party.

Grandma was going to turn eighty-two on Friday. I heard Mom ordering a cake from the bakery over the phone. "Don't put any icing on it," she said. "Just a plain angel cake, as light as you can make it."

When I opened the refrigerator Thursday after school, I spotted a green plastic basket of plump strawberries that my mother must have driven across town to buy at the specialty market. A carton of whipping cream stood next to the strawberries.

Grandma would enjoy her cake, all right. Angel cake with fresh strawberries was her favorite.

So Mom was ready. I should mention that Grandma was my dad's mother, not my mom's. Mom tried to be nice to Grandma, but it wasn't as if they were best friends.

That afternoon when Dad came home, he showed me the phone he had bought for Grandma. "It has speed-dialing," he said. "She won't have to push so many buttons when she calls the doctor's office or her sister." Dad looked pleased. "Her fingers are so stiff with arthritis that the phone seemed a good idea."

But what about me? Here I was with only one dollar in my pocket and one night to think of a gift. Even though Mom always insisted that "it's the thought that counts," I had a big problem. My mind was even more empty of ideas than my wallet was empty of money.

When I have a problem, it sometimes helps to shoot a few baskets in the driveway. For some reason, hearing the old basketball smack against the blacktop or bounce off the rim gets my mind going when it seems stalled.

So, even though it was February and frosty, I zipped my jacket and stepped outside. "Close that door tight behind you," I heard

Grandma shout. She had a thing about closing doors.

Dribble, shoot, rebound. For a while I just played without even trying to think.

I began to remember back before Granddad died, when we used to visit them in Kentucky. Granddad showed me how to do a jump shot, in fact. I was too short then to have any hopes of making a basket, but he just said, "Don't worry. You'll grow. Just like your father. The important thing is to get the skills down so when you do grow, you'll be ready to play."

Thinking about Granddad made me sigh. Grandma hadn't been so crabby when he was alive. I guess her life was a lot happier then.

Swish! I'd made two in a row.

I remembered a green glass dish in the shape of a leaf that Grandma used to keep on a table back in Kentucky. It was always full of those red-and-white-striped peppermint candies with the cellophane twisted on either side. I hadn't thought of that dish for a long time. Maybe it was lost or broken when Dad rented the truck and brought Grandma and the belongings we had room for up here to Ohio.

Just thinking about that candy dish made me taste the peppermint slowly dissolving on my tongue. I could almost hear Grandma saying, "Help yourself to a piece of peppermint, Burt. Take two if you want." That voice had a smile behind it. It was a voice I hadn't heard in a long time.

Aha! I took one last shot, then dribbled to the back door, ran up the steps two at a time, and grabbed my wallet. At the drugstore I found candies just

like the ones I'd remembered. They were two for a nickel. I bought a whole dollar's worth.

When I got home, I had my second inspiration. I pulled a large curled leaf from the rhododendron bush in our side yard. It was almost exactly the size of Grandma's old candy dish.

The next night, after the cake, came the time for presents.

"You just ate my present," Mom announced.

Grandma actually smiled. "I surely did enjoy it, too. Thank you, Eleanor."

Then my dad brought out the telephone. Grandma didn't do as well with that. Nothing Dad did for her ever seemed quite right. "Another newfangled gadget," she said. "Really, James. You know I never did like gadgets. I'll never figure out how to use this."

She pushed the phone aside. Everyone was quiet.

I took a deep breath. "Grandma," I began, "I've got something for you. I know it isn't much, but I hope you'll like it."

I got up from my chair and placed the leaf with the candies tucked inside right on Grandma's place mat. Grandma, Mom, and Dad all looked at me a bit strangely. I decided to explain.

"Remember when we used to visit you in Kentucky?" I said.

"The first thing I'd do was take a peppermint out of that green-leaf dish in the front hall—after hugging you and Granddad, of course."

I looked at Grandma. Her eyes were red and watery, but her mouth turned up at the corners as she said quietly, as if from far away, "Why, yes, Burt. I remember that dish well. It didn't survive the move....I guess a lot of things didn't survive

the move. But thank you for remembering it."

Silence swamped us again, but a different kind of silence. I saw Dad catch Mom's eyes, and they both looked down at their plates.

Grandma spoke next. It was the old voice, the one with the smile in it.

"Here," she said, "would everyone like to take a peppermint? Take two if you want."

And we all did, starting with my dad.

1.   What is Burt's main problem in the story?

Ⓐ   He does not get along with Grandma.

Ⓑ   He is too short to make a basket.

Ⓒ   He needs to think of a gift for Grandma's birthday.

Ⓓ   His dad and mom don't talk to him much.

FollowThese Steps   The question asks for Burt's main problem in the story. Burt tells you what his problem is. Do you remember it? If not, read the section where Burt talks about his problem.

2.   According to the story, why is Grandma so grouchy?

Ⓐ   She does not like Burt's mom.

Ⓑ   She is angry that she is in a wheelchair.

Ⓒ   She fears growing older.

Ⓓ   She misses Granddad.

FollowThese Steps   The answer to this question is not stated right in the story, but you can figure it out. Look back at the part of the story when Burt remembers back before Granddad died. How did Grandma act when Granddad was alive? How does she act now? What do you think makes her grouchy?

3. In paragraph 18, Burt says, "When I got home, I had my second inspiration." What is the **best** meaning of the word *inspiration* in this story?

Ⓐ sad thought

Ⓑ exciting, happy adventure

Ⓒ scary dream

Ⓓ sudden, bright idea

Follow These Steps This question asks you to find the meaning of a word you might not know. To do this, you must look at how the word is used in the story. First, read the sentence in which the word appears. If you still don't know the meaning, go back and read the surrounding sentences. They might help you figure it out. As a check, replace the word in the story with each choice. The one that makes the most sense is probably the answer.

4. Why does Grandma have the voice "with the smile in it" at the end of the story?

Ⓐ She is happy that Burt's mom gave her a nice cake.

Ⓑ Burt's gift reminds her of happier times.

Ⓒ She likes Dad's thoughtful gift.

Ⓓ She likes birthday parties.

Follow These Steps Think about all that has happened in the story. How does Grandma treat her family? Why is Grandma crabby? What gift does Burt decide to give Grandma? How does Grandma act after she gets this gift?

5. Why is the title of this story called "The Thought That Counted"? Use details from the story to support your answer.

Follow These Steps   For this question, begin by thinking about what the title means. What was the thought behind Burt's gift? Why does it "count" so much to Grandma? You might want to jot down your ideas on scrap paper before you begin to write. Try to put your ideas in the order in which you want to write about them. You might use an outline to organize your thoughts. After you finish your essay, check your work to make sure your writing is the best it can be.

Write your answer on the lines below.

_____

_____

_____

_____

_____

_____

_____

_____

_____

_____

_____

_____

_____

6. Below is a time line of events for "The Thought That Counted." Some important events have been filled in for you. Two important events are missing.

Read the events that have been filled in. Then, decide what important events are missing. Fill in each empty box with what you think is the most important event that belongs there.

Time Line for "The Thought That Counted"

Burt needs to think of a gift for Grandma's birthday.

↓

Burt remembers a leaf candy dish that Grandma kept on a table when Granddad was alive.

↓

↓

Burt gives Grandma the gift and explains its meaning.

↓

↓

7. Choose one of the events you wrote for the time line. Explain why you think this event is important to the story. Use details from the story to support your answer.

Write your answer on the lines below.

_____

_____

_____

_____

_____

_____

_____

_____

_____

_____

_____

_____

_____

_____

_____

_____

_____

CHAPTER Seven
Everyday Text

How Do You Read Everyday Text?

You can find examples of everyday text all around you. In the classroom, you'll find everyday text in the class rules on the wall and the homework assignment on the board. Outside of school, you can find everyday text in recipes, directions, and letters. Everyday text might contain pictures or charts. When you read everyday text, you'll find it helpful to do the following:

◆ **Find the main idea** The main idea is the point the writer wants to make about a topic. Sometimes, it is easier to find the main idea if you first know the purpose. For example, the purpose of a recipe for chocolate cookies is to teach the reader how to make the cookies. The main idea is that following the writer's directions will result in tasty chocolate cookies.

◆ **See how the parts make up the whole** Often everyday text will give instructions or steps to follow. See how each step will help you do something.

◆ **Look at the order** In everyday text, order is very important. For example, a time order will help you follow steps that teach you how to do something.

Directions: Read the text. Then, answer the questions that follow.

Kite

by Alice Gilbreath

To make a kite, you will need these things:

◆ a plastic bread bag

◆ string

◆ scissors

When you have all these things, follow these steps:

1. Fold the open end of the bread bag.

   Make the fold as wide as three fingers.

   With your fingers, pinch along the fold.

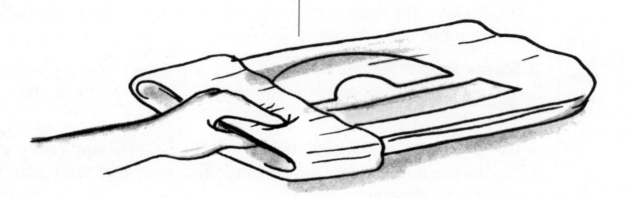

2. With your scissors, snip a hole through the bread bag.

Snip through the folded part.

Snip through both sides of the folded part.

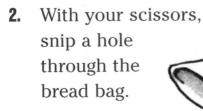

3. Cut a piece of string longer than your arm.

Put the string through both sides of the hole.

Tie the string near the fold.

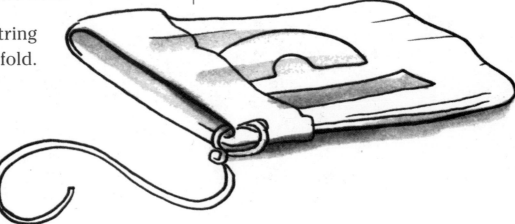

4. Make two more holes
in the bread bag.

Make them the same way.

Cut two more pieces of string.

Cut them the same way.

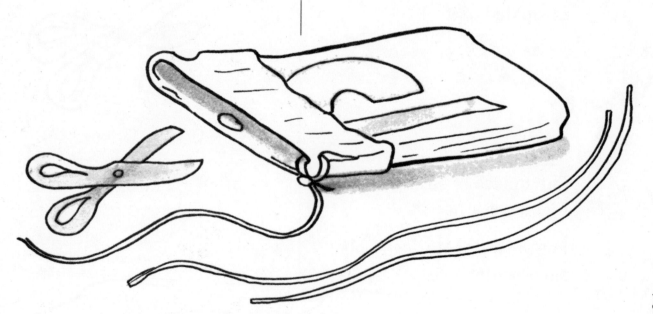

5. Put the pieces of string in the holes.

Put them in the same way.

Tie the pieces of string.

Tie them the same way.

Now you have three pieces of string tied through the bread bag.

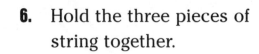

6. Hold the three pieces of string together.

Tie a knot at the ends of the strings.

Tie the strings together.

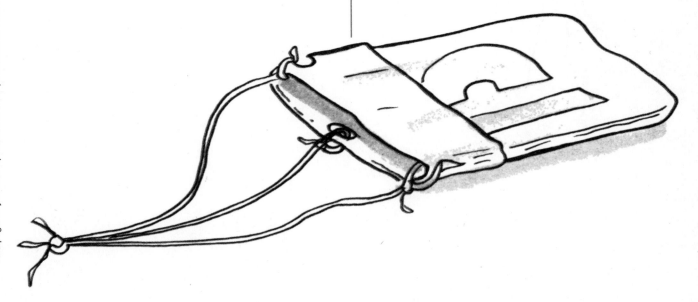

7. Your kite is finished.

Hold your kite by the knot.

Run into the wind.

The wind will make your kite fly.

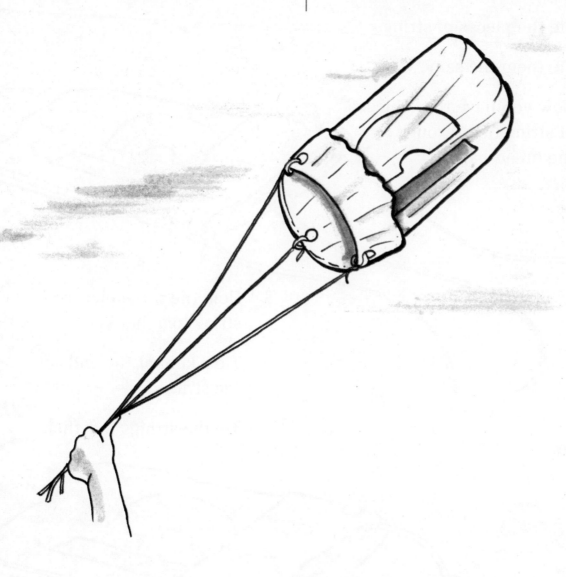

1. **In step 2, you snip through the folded part of the bread bag. The word *snip* means**

   (A) cut in short, quick strokes.

   (B) pinch with your fingers.

   (C) tie a knot with string.

   (D) tear with your hands.

Follow These Steps Look back at step 2. Read the step. Look at the illustration. What are you doing when you snip through the folded part of the bread bag?

2. **The string is attached to the bread bag with**

   (A) glue.

   (B) tape.

   (C) knots.

   (D) staples.

Follow These Steps The answer to this question is right in the text. How are all of the strings attached to the bread bag? If you don't remember, glance through the text and look at the drawings.

3. **Which of the following must come first?**

(A) Hold the three pieces of string together.

(B) Put the pieces of string in the holes.

(C) Run into the wind with the kite.

(D) Hold your kite by the knot.

Follow These Steps   Reread steps 5, 6, and 7. All of the sentences tell things you must do in these steps. Which is the first thing you must do?

4. **What is the main purpose of the knot at the ends of the three strings?**

(A) It keeps the strings from falling off of the bread bag.

(B) It makes the kite look good.

(C) It makes the kite fly.

(D) It gives you a fixed place to hold onto the kite.

Follow These Steps   Look back at steps 6 and 7. Look at the drawings that go with these steps. What is the purpose of the knot?

5. Suppose you want your kite to fly higher. What would you do?

Follow These Steps Think about what is attached to the kite. Look at the steps again. What could you change to make your kite fly higher in the air?

Write your answer on the lines below.

_____

_____

_____

_____

_____

_____

_____

_____

_____

_____

_____

_____

_____

_____

6. Mei Li lives in China. She has a plastic dragon that she wants to make into a kite to fly on Kites' Day. She has already folded up the end of the dragon and snipped holes through the folded part. Write down the next four steps for Mei Li to follow. You can skip the explanations and just list the steps.

Write your response in the boxes below.

1	2	3
Fold the open end.	Snip a hole.	_____ _____ _____ _____

4	5	6
_____ _____ _____	_____ _____ _____	_____ _____ _____

Follow These Steps   Look at the way the first two steps are written. You can write the next four steps in the same way. You do not need to write out the whole explanation. Just write down each step and leave out the instructions that tell you how to do each one.

UNIT 3 Practice Test

You will now be taking a practice test. This test will include all the skills you have read about in this book. Follow the directions in each part. Read each question carefully, and think about your answer. You may look back at the reading passages as needed.

For the multiple-choice questions, work carefully and try to get as many questions right as you can. Don't spend too much time on any one question. If you don't know an answer, make the best choice you can. Then go on to the next question. If there's time at the end of a part, you can go back and check your work in that part only.

For the open-ended questions, plan out what you want to say before writing. Make sure that you answer all parts of the question. After you complete your draft, be sure to revise and edit your writing.

PRACTICE Test

Day 1

Directions

You will now be taking a practice test. You will be asked to write, read passages, and answer questions.

Remember the following points:

1. Be sure to write your answers neatly on the lines given.

2. You may look over your work only in the part you are working in.

3. A STOP sign at the bottom of a page means you must **not** turn the page unless you are told to do so.

GO ON TO THE NEXT PAGE ➡

ESPA Success in Language Arts Literacy ◆ LEVEL C

Writing Task A

Use the picture on page 68 to write a story about what might be happening.

You may take notes, create an idea web, make a story map, or do other prewriting work on page 69. Then, write your story on page 70.

Here is a writing checklist to help you do your best writing. Before you begin writing, read the checklist.

Writer's Checklist

❏ Know your audience.

❏ Think about your topic and reason for writing.

❏ Show your audience that your point of view is correct.

❏ Support your point of view with details and other information.

❏ Organize your ideas so that they make sense.

❏ State your ideas clearly.

❏ Use different vocabulary words.

❏ Write neatly.

After you write your story, read it to yourself. Go over the checklist to make sure that your writing is the best it can be.

TURN TO THE NEXT PAGE ➡

GO ON TO THE NEXT PAGE ➡

Writing Task A — Prewriting Space

Use this space to plan your writing.

TURN TO THE NEXT PAGE ➡

Writing Task A

_____

_____

_____

_____

_____

_____

_____

_____

_____

_____

_____

_____

_____

_____

_____

_____

_____

_____

_____

**DO NOT GO ON
UNTIL YOU ARE
TOLD TO DO SO.**

If you have time, you may look over your work in this part only.

Directions

Now you will read a story that someone else has written about the picture. Then, answer the questions that follow.

The questions will be either multiple-choice or open-ended.

1. You may look over the story as often as you wish.

2. Read the questions carefully, and think about your answer.

3. For multiple-choice questions, choose the best answer, and fill in the circle next to your choice. Check that you have filled in the correct circle.

4. Go on to the next question if you do not know an answer. Later, if you have time, you may go back to the skipped question.

Sample Story

The following story and questions are a sample to show you what the questions will be like and how to mark your answer.

Two men came upon a bear. Quick as a flash, one of the men climbed the nearest tree and hid in the branches. The second man had not been so quick in his thinking. He fell to the ground and hoped for the best.

The bear walked over and poked the man with his snout and sniffed. The man held his breath and pretended to be dead. Then the bear turned and went back into the forest. It is said that a bear will not touch a dead body.

TURN TO THE NEXT PAGE ➡

Sample Multiple-Choice Question

Choose the best answer. Fill in the circle next to the answer you choose. For example:

In the story, where are the two men?

Ⓐ on a lake

Ⓑ in the desert

● in the woods

Ⓓ in the city

The correct answer is C. The circle with the C in it is filled to show you that C is the correct answer.

Sample Open-Ended Question

To answer the question, you must write several sentences on the lines provided. For example:

Do you think the two men will remain friends? Be sure to use examples or ideas from the story to support your answer.

I think that the second man will stop being friends with the first man.

He will be angry that his friend saved himself and didn't help save him.

[These are the first two sentences of a good answer.]

GO ON TO THE NEXT PAGE ➡

Directions: Read the story. Then, answer the questions that follow.

A Gift for Tía Rosa

by Karen T. Taha

"Around, over, through, and pull. Around, over, through, and pull," Carmela repeated as she knitted. A rainbow of red, orange, and gold wool stretched almost to her feet. Now and then she stopped and listened for her father's car. He mustn't see what she was knitting!

The rumble of a motor made her drop the needles and run to the window. In the gray November shadows, she saw a battered brown station wagon turn into the garage next door.

"Mamá, she's home! Tía Rosa is home!" Carmela called. Carmela's mother hurried out of the bedroom. She put her arm around Carmela. They watched as lights flickered on in the windows, bringing the neat white house back to life.

"I know you want to see Tía Rosa, Carmela," said her mother, "but she and Tío Juan have had a long trip. Tía Rosa must be very tired after two weeks in the hospital."

"But can I call her, Mamá?" asked Carmela. "The scarf for Papá is almost done. She promised to help me fringe it when she came home."

TURN TO THE NEXT PAGE ➡

"No, Carmela. Not now," her mother replied firmly. "Tía Rosa needs to rest." She smoothed back Carmela's thick black hair from her face.

Carmela tossed her head. "But Mamá . . . !"

"No, Carmela!"

Carmela knew there was no use arguing. But it wasn't fair. Tomorrow she would have to go to school. She couldn't see Tía Rosa until the afternoon. Her mother just didn't understand.

Frowning, Carmela plopped back on the sofa and picked up the silver knitting needles. At least she would finish more of the scarf before Tía Rosa saw it tomorrow. She bent over her knitting and began once more. "Around, over, through, and pull." The phone rang in the kitchen.

(11) "I'll get it!" Carmela shouted, bounding into the hall. "Hello?" Her dark eyes sparkled. "Tía Rosa! You must see Papá's scarf. It's almost finished . . . You did? For me? Okay, I'll be right there!"

The phone clattered as Carmela hung up. "Mamá! Tía Rosa wants to see the scarf. She even brought me a surprise!"

Carmela's mother smiled and shook her head. "Tía Rosa is unbelievable."

Carmela stuffed the bright wool into her school bag. "I'm going to make Tía Rosa a surprise after I finish Papá's scarf!" she called as she ran out.

She ran across the yard to Tía Rosa's front door. The door swung open, and there was Tío Juan. He looked taller and thinner than she remembered, and his eyes looked sad.

Tío Juan was as tall as Tía Rosa was short, Carmela thought. He was as thin as Tía Rosa was plump. And he was as good at listening as Tía Rosa was at talking.

"*Hola,*[1] Carmelita," he said, bending to kiss her cheek. He led her down the hall. "Tía Rosa is sitting up in bed. She's tired, but she wanted to see her favorite neighbor."

---

1. **Hola:** the Spanish word for *hello*

GO ON TO THE NEXT PAGE ➡

ESPA Success in Language Arts Literacy ◆ LEVEL C

Tía Rosa in bed! In all her eight years Carmela had never seen Tía Rosa sick. She held her breath and peeked into the bedroom. Tía Rosa's round face crinkled into a smile when she saw Carmela.

"Carmelita, come give me a hug!"

Hugging Tía Rosa always made Carmela feel safe and warm. Tía Rosa was like a soft pillow that smelled of soap and bath powder and sometimes of sweet tamales. Now there was another smell, a dentist office smell, Carmela decided.

"Carmelita, I've missed you!" said Tía Rosa. "Let's look at what you have knitted."

Carmela handed her the scarf. Tía Rosa smiled. "Your papá will be proud to wear it," she said. "Tomorrow I'll show you how to fringe it, and I will start on the pink baby blanket for my granddaughter!"

Carmela laughed. "How do you know that Pepe's wife will have a girl?" she asked. Pepe was the oldest of Tía Rosa's six sons.

"Because," answered Tía Rosa with a grin, "anyone who has six sons and no daughters, deserves a granddaughter!"

"But Tía Rosa, what if the baby is a boy? Won't you love him just the same?"

"Of course," laughed Tía Rosa.

Carmela knew Tía Rosa would love the baby, boy or girl, but she crossed her fingers and wished for a girl, too.

"Now for the surprise!" said Tía Rosa. She handed Carmela a small white box. "Go on now. See what's inside."

Carmela opened the box carefully. A snowy ball of cotton lay inside. As she pulled at the cotton, her fingers touched something hard and very small. She heard the "clish" of a chain as she lifted the surprise from under the cotton. In her hand Carmela held a tiny silver rose on a fine chain.

"Oh, Tía Rosa. It's beautiful!" exclaimed Carmela.

"The rose is so you'll remember your old Tía Rosa," she said.

"How could I forget you, Tía Rosa?" asked Carmela. "You're right here!"

Before she went home, Carmela put the rose around her neck. She

TURN TO THE NEXT PAGE ➡

This page may not be reproduced without permission of Steck-Vaughn/Berrent.

promised to return the next day after school.

Carmela returned the next day, and the next, and every day for a whole week. Tía Rosa stayed in her room, and Tío Juan moved a chair by the bed for Carmela. Together the two friends worked on their surprise gifts.

"Why does Tía Rosa stay in bed all the time?" Carmela asked her father at breakfast one day.

Her father looked away for a moment. Then he took Carmela's hands in his. "Tía Rosa is very sick, Carmela. The doctors don't think she can get well," he explained.

"But Papá," said Carmela. "I have been sick lots of times. Remember when Tía Rosa stayed with me when you and Mamá had to go away?"

"Yes," answered her father. "But Tía Rosa . . ."

GO ON TO THE NEXT PAGE ➡

ESPA Success in Language Arts Literacy ♦ LEVEL C

Carmela didn't listen. "Now I will stay with Tía Rosa until she gets well, too," she said.

Every afternoon Carmela worked on her father's scarf. The fringe was the easiest part. With Tía Rosa's help she would have the scarf finished long before Christmas.

Tía Rosa worked on the pink baby blanket, but the needles didn't fly in her sure brown fingers like they once did. Carmela teased her. "Tía Rosa, are you knitting slowly because you might have to change the pink yarn to blue when the baby is born?"

"No, no," replied Tía Rosa with a grin. "The baby will surely be a girl. We need girls in this family. You're the only one I have!"

Sometimes Tía Rosa fell asleep with her knitting still in her hands. Then Carmela would quietly put the needles and yarn into Tía Rosa's big green knitting bag and tiptoe out of the room.

Carmela liked Saturdays and Sundays best because she could spend more time at Tía Rosa's.

Mamá always sent a plate of cookies with her, and Tío Juan made hot chocolate for them.

One Saturday morning when Carmela rang the doorbell, Tío Juan didn't come. Carmela ran to the garage and peeked in the window. The brown station wagon was gone.

She returned home and called Tía Rosa's number. The phone rang and rang. Carmela went down the steps to the basement. Her mother was rubbing stain into freshly sanded wood of an old desk.

"Tía Rosa isn't home," said Carmela sadly. Her mother looked up from her work.

"I thought I heard a car in the night," said her mother. "Surely Tío Juan would have called us if . . ."

Just then the phone rang upstairs. Carmela heard footsteps creak across the floor as her father walked to answer it.

Moments later the footsteps thumped softly towards the basement door. Carmela's father came slowly down the steps. Carmela shivered when she saw

TURN TO THE NEXT PAGE ➡

his sad face. He put his arms around Carmela and her mother and hugged them close. "Tía Rosa is gone," he whispered. "She died early this morning."

No, her father's words couldn't be true. Carmela didn't believe it. Tía Rosa would come back. She had always come back before.

"It's not true!" cried Carmela. She broke away from her mother and father and raced up the stairs. She ran out the front door and through the yard to Tía Rosa's house. She pushed the doorbell again and again. She pounded on the silent door until her fists hurt. At last she sank down on the steps.

Later, her father came. With a soft hanky, he brushed the tears from her cheeks. At last, they walked quietly home.

The next days were long and lonely for Carmela. She didn't care that Papá's finished scarf lay

hidden in her closet, bright and beautiful. She didn't want to see it. She didn't want to feel the cool, smooth knitting needles in her hands ever again.

The white house next door was busy with people coming and going. Carmela took over food her mother and father cooked, but she quickly

GO ON TO THE NEXT PAGE ➡

returned home. She didn't like to see Tío Juan. Seeing Tío Juan made her miss Tía Rosa even more.

One day Carmela said to her mother, "Tía Rosa died before I could give her anything, Mamá. She baked me cookies and taught me to knit and brought me surprises. I was going to surprise her. Now it's too late."

"Carmela, Tía Rosa didn't want her kindness returned. She wanted it passed on," said her mother. "That way a part of Tía Rosa will never die."

"But I wanted to give something to her!" shouted Carmela. "Just to Tía Rosa. To show her that I loved her!"

"She knew that, Carmela. Every smile and hug and visit told her that you loved her," said her mother. "Now it's Tío Juan who needs our love."

"I know," answered Carmela in a soft voice, "but it's hard, Mamá. It hurts so much without Tía Rosa."

One night Carmela's mother asked Tío Juan to dinner. Carmela met him at the door. This time Carmela did not turn away when she saw his sad eyes. Instead, she hugged him tightly.

For the first time in a week, Tío Juan smiled. "Carmelita, tomorrow you must come next door. I would like you to meet my new granddaughter. Her parents have named her Rosita, little Rose, after her grandmother."

Carmela looked down at her silver rose necklace so Tío Juan would not see the tears in her eyes. Tía Rosa knew the baby would be a girl. Then Carmela remembered the unfinished blanket. "Now I know what I can give!" she said.

After dinner Tío Juan went back to the white house. A few minutes later he returned with Tía Rosa's big knitting bag. Very carefully Carmela pulled out the half-finished blanket and wound the soft pink yarn around the needle.

"Around, over, through, and pull. Around, over, through, and pull." Carmela smiled. At last she had a gift for Tía Rosa.

◆ ◆ ◆

TURN TO THE NEXT PAGE ➡

1. Read this sentence from paragraph 11 in the story.
   "I'll get it!" Carmela shouted, bounding into the hall.
   The <u>best</u> meaning of the word *bounding* is

   Ⓐ frowning.

   Ⓑ rolling.

   Ⓒ leaping.

   Ⓓ playing.

2. What do Carmela and Tía Rosa do together?

   Ⓐ play cards

   Ⓑ watch television

   Ⓒ knit

   Ⓓ paint

GO ON TO THE NEXT PAGE ➡

3. **What is Carmela's problem, or conflict?**

Ⓐ   She can't finish a scarf for her father's Christmas gift.

Ⓑ   She fears that her visits are tiring Tía Rosa.

Ⓒ   She does not get along well with Tío Juan.

Ⓓ   She has trouble dealing with Tía Rosa's death.

4. **What is Carmela's gift for Tía Rosa?**

Ⓐ   She will finish the blanket for Tía Rosa's granddaughter.

Ⓑ   She will give Tío Juan the silver rose necklace.

Ⓒ   She will bring flowers to Tía Rosa's grave.

Ⓓ   She will knit a scarf for Tía Rosa's son.

TURN TO THE NEXT PAGE ➡

5. Do you think that Tía Rosa would like Carmela's gift? Why or why not?

Write your answer on the lines below.

_____

_____

_____

_____

_____

_____

_____

_____

_____

_____

_____

_____

_____

_____

_____

_____

GO ON TO THE NEXT PAGE ➡

6. Choose <u>two</u> words that best describe Tía Rosa from the box below.

kind	afraid	wise
mean	thoughtful	skillful
brave	loving	funny

Write a word in each of the top boxes. Then, in the box below it, give an example from the story that shows how Tía Rosa is like the word.

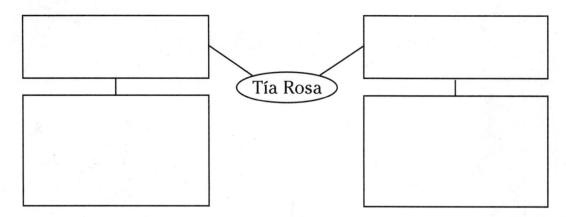

Tell how each word you chose <u>best</u> describes Tía Rosa. Use details from the story to support your answer.

Write your answer on the lines below.

_____

_____

_____

_____

_____

_____

_____

DO NOT GO ON UNTIL YOU ARE TOLD TO DO SO.

If you have time, you may look over your work in this part only.

Directions: Read the poem, "The Pasture," to yourself while it is read to you. Then, you will complete a writing task. Ideas from the poem may help you with your writing.

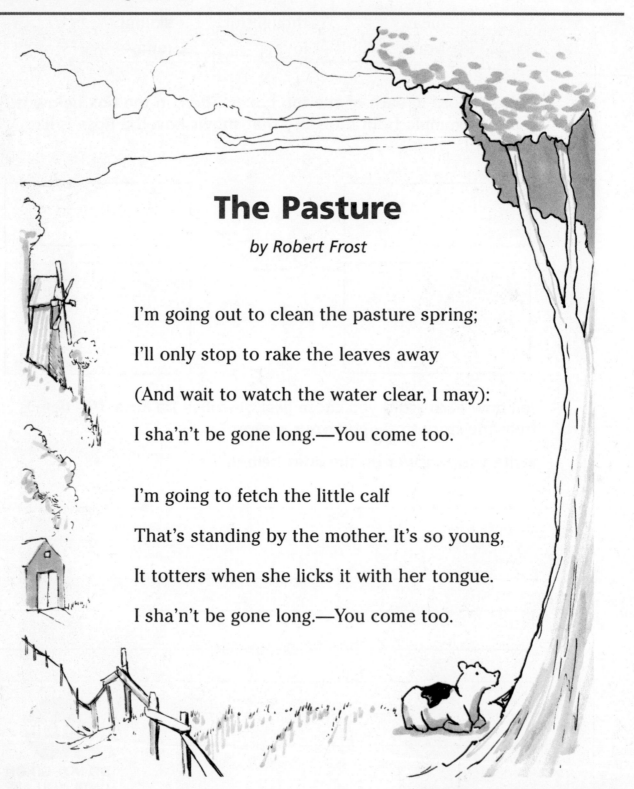

The Pasture

by Robert Frost

I'm going out to clean the pasture spring;

I'll only stop to rake the leaves away

(And wait to watch the water clear, I may):

I sha'n't be gone long.—You come too.

I'm going to fetch the little calf

That's standing by the mother. It's so young,

It totters when she licks it with her tongue.

I sha'n't be gone long.—You come too.

GO ON TO THE NEXT PAGE ➡

Writing Task B

Most people don't like doing chores. But, there are ways to make chores more enjoyable. Think about a chore you do. How could you make it more enjoyable? Could you think about it in a different way? Could you have someone keep you company while you do it? Or, is there some other way to help you enjoy your work? Write a composition about your ideas. Be sure to explain your chore, what don't you like about it, and what you could do to make it more enjoyable.

You may take notes, create an idea web, or do other prewriting work in the space on page 86. Then, write your composition on page 87.

Use the following checklist to help you do your best writing. Before you begin writing, read the checklist.

Writer's Checklist

- ❑ Know your audience.
- ❑ Think about your topic and reason for writing.
- ❑ Show your audience that your point of view is correct.
- ❑ Support your point of view with details and other information.
- ❑ Organize your ideas so that they make sense.
- ❑ State your ideas clearly.
- ❑ Use different vocabulary words.
- ❑ Write neatly.

After you write your composition, read it to yourself. Go over the checklist to make sure that your writing is the best it can be.

TURN TO THE NEXT PAGE ➡

Writing Task B — Prewriting Space

Use this space to plan your writing.

GO ON TO THE NEXT PAGE ➡

ESPA Success in Language Arts Literacy ◆ LEVEL C

Writing Task B

_____

_____

_____

_____

_____

_____

_____

_____

_____

_____

_____

_____

_____

_____

_____

_____

_____

**DO NOT GO ON
UNTIL YOU ARE
TOLD TO DO SO.**

If you have time, you may look over your work in this part only.

PRACTICE Test
Day 2

Directions

In the next part, you will read everyday text and then answer the questions that follow. The questions will be either multiple-choice or open-ended.

Sample Story

The following story and questions are a sample to show you what the questions will be like and how to mark your answer.

Two men came upon a bear. Quick as a flash, one of the men climbed the nearest tree and hid in the branches. The second man had not been so quick in his thinking. He fell to the ground and hoped for the best.

The bear walked over and poked the man with his snout and sniffed. The man held his breath and pretended to be dead. Then the bear turned and went back into the forest. It is said that a bear will not touch a dead body.

◆ ◆ ◆

GO ON TO THE NEXT PAGE

ESPA Success in Language Arts Literacy ◆ LEVEL C

Sample Multiple-Choice Question

Choose the best answer. Fill in the circle next to the answer you choose. For example:

Why did the second man "hope for the best"?

Ⓐ   He hoped the first man would not hurt him.

Ⓑ   He hoped the first man would fall out of the tree.

●   He hoped the bear would not hurt him.

Ⓓ   He hoped the tree branches would hide him from the bear.

The correct answer is C. The circle with the C in it is filled to show you that C is the correct answer.

Sample Open-Ended Question

To answer the question, you must write several sentences on the lines provided. For example:

Do you think the two men will remain friends? Be sure to use examples or ideas from the story to support your answer.

I think that the first man will remain friends with the second man.

He will do what is best for himself.

[These are the first two sentences of a good answer.]

TURN TO THE NEXT PAGE ➡

Directions: Read the text. Then, answer the questions that follow.

Disappearing Coin Trick

Make a coin disappear right before your friends' eyes.

by the editors of Owl *magazine*

You'll need:

◆ Old clear drinking glass

◆ Newspaper

◆ Construction paper

◆ Pencil

◆ Scissors

◆ Glue

◆ Coin

◆ Scarf

The Setup:

1. Trace around the rim of the glass on a piece of construction paper and cut out the paper circle.

GO ON TO THE NEXT PAGE ➡

2. Squeeze some glue on newspaper and dip the rim of the glass into it.

3. Place the glue-rimmed glass rim-side down on the paper circle. Let it dry.

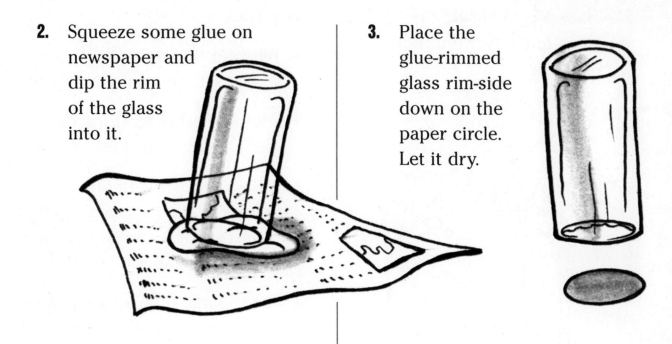

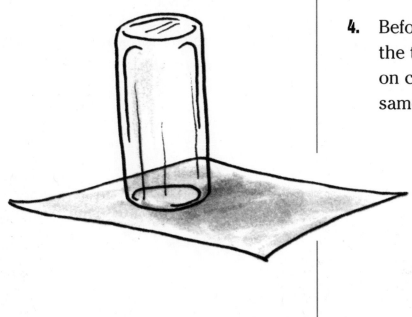

4. Before your friends arrive, put the trick glass circle-side down on construction paper of the same color as the circle.

TURN TO THE NEXT PAGE ➡

5. Place a coin beside the glass, and cover the trick with a scarf.

The Trick:

◆ Tell your friends that you are going to make a coin disappear.

◆ Lift the scarf to let the audience see the glass and coin.

◆ Wave the scarf with one hand in front of the glass and chant: "Abracadabra, abracadoo. I am amazing and so are you."

◆ At the same time, quickly slide the glass over the coin with your other hand. Whip the scarf away as you shout "Ta da!" The coin "disappears"!

◆ Now make the coin reappear the same way.

◆ Practice the trick until you can do it perfectly.

◆ ◆ ◆

GO ON TO THE NEXT PAGE ➡

7. What part of the glass is the *rim*?

    Ⓐ left side

    Ⓑ top edge

    Ⓒ bottom edge

    Ⓓ right side

8. Before you dip the rim of the glass into the glue, you squeeze some glue on the

    Ⓐ newspaper.

    Ⓑ scarf.

    Ⓒ construction paper.

    Ⓓ table.

TURN TO THE NEXT PAGE ➡

9. The coin "disappears" because it is

   Ⓐ on the floor.

   Ⓑ hidden up your sleeve.

   Ⓒ under the construction paper on the rim.

   Ⓓ in the scarf.

10. This text is ordered by showing

    Ⓐ steps in a certain order to fix a problem.

    Ⓑ steps in a certain order to teach something.

    Ⓒ how things are alike and different.

    Ⓓ how one thing causes another to happen.

GO ON TO THE NEXT PAGE ➡

◇ ◇ ◇

ESPA Success in Language Arts Literacy ♦ LEVEL C

11. Why is the scarf used? Why is it important to the trick? Explain
     your answer.

     Write your answer on the lines below.

     _____

     _____

     _____

     _____

     _____

     _____

     _____

     _____

     _____

     _____

     _____

     _____

     _____

     _____

     _____

TURN TO THE NEXT PAGE ➡

◆ ◆ ◆

12. You decide to perform the "Disappearing Coin Trick" for your class. You bring the trick glass and construction paper with you to school. But you forgot to bring the scarf and the coin. What can you use instead of the scarf and the coin? Think about the kinds of things you might find in your classroom. Choose two things then rewrite the trick using these two new things.

Write your answer on the lines below.

_____

_____

_____

_____

_____

_____

_____

_____

_____

_____

_____

_____

_____

_____

If you have time, you may look over your work in this part only.

ESPA Success in Language Arts Literacy ◆ LEVEL C